SPORTS CODING CONCEPTS

# SPORTY CONDITIONALS

Allyssa Loya

Lerner Publications ◆ Minneapolis

Lerner Publications Company
An imprint of Lerner Publishing Group, Inc.
241 First Avenue North
Minneapolis, MN 55401 USA

For reading levels and more information, look up this title at www.lernerbooks.com.

Main body text set in Mikado a Regular.
Typeface provided by HVD Fonts.

**Library of Congress Cataloging-in-Publication Data**

Names: Loya, Allyssa, author.
Title: Sporty conditionals / Allyssa Loya.
Description: Minneapolis : Lerner Publications, [2020] | Series: Sports coding concepts | Includes bibliographical references and index. | Audience: Ages 7–9. | Audience: Grades K to 3. | Summary: "Learn about conditionals in a fun sports adventure for readers not yet ready for coding on computers. Sports-themed projects encourage readers to actively engage with the content and learn about the basics of coding" —Provided by publisher.
Identifiers: LCCN 2019013122 (print) | LCCN 2019980090 (ebook) | ISBN 9781541576926 (lb : alk. paper) | ISBN 9781541583641 (ebook)
Subjects: LCSH: Sports—Juvenile literature. | Coding theory—Juvenile literature.
Classification: LCC GV705.4 .L69 2020 (print) | LCC GV705.4 (ebook) | DDC 796—dc23

LC record available at https://lccn.loc.gov/2019013122
LC ebook record available at https://lccn.loc.gov/2019980090

Manufactured in the United States of America
1-46711-47705-7/31/2019

# Table of Contents

Sports and Conditionals . . . . . . . . . . . . 4
Hands Up! Hands Out!. . . . . . . . . . . . . . . .6
Victory Dance . . . . . . . . . . . . . . . . . . . . . 8
Good Catch!. . . . . . . . . . . . . . . . . . . . . . .10
Up and Over . . . . . . . . . . . . . . . . . . . . . .12
Block That Shot! . . . . . . . . . . . . . . . . . . .14
Into the End Zone . . . . . . . . . . . . . . . . . .16
Looped Leaps . . . . . . . . . . . . . . . . . . . . .18
The White Flag Is Up!. . . . . . . . . . . . . . . 20
On the Slopes . . . . . . . . . . . . . . . . . . . . .22
Hit or Miss . . . . . . . . . . . . . . . . . . . . . . . 24

Keep Coding . . . . . . . . . . . . . . . . . . . . . . . . . . . . . . . . 28
Answer Key . . . . . . . . . . . . . . . . . . . . . . . . . . . . . . . . . 29
Glossary . . . . . . . . . . . . . . . . . . . . . . . . . . . . . . . . . . . 30
Further Information . . . . . . . . . . . . . . . . . . . . . . . . . . 31
Index. . . . . . . . . . . . . . . . . . . . . . . . . . . . . . . . . . . . . . . 32

# SPORTS AND CONDITIONALS

**If athletes were computers, lines of code could tell them how to play. Lines of code are instructions that tell computers what to do. An algorithm is many lines of code put together.**

Code also tells computers how to make choices. Imagine a soccer player running with the ball. If she's near the net, she should shoot the ball. If she's not, she should pass. In coding, choices like these are called conditionals. Conditionals are lines of code that tell computers what to do based on different conditions.

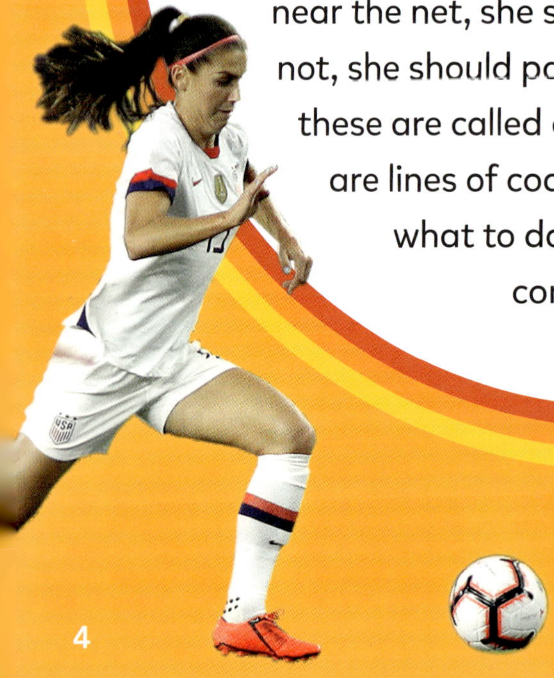

You will need plenty of paper, a pencil, a die, and a pair of scissors for some of the activities in this book.

# HANDS UP! HANDS OUT!

In basketball, defenders try to take the ball. If a player from the other team is dribbling, defenders put their hands out to the sides. If a player is about to shoot, defenders put their hands up in the air.

Find a partner. Pretend you have the ball and your partner is on defense. If you are dribbling, your partner should put their hands out. If you are shooting, your partner should block.

Defenders follow these conditionals:

**Is your partner dribbling? If yes, put your hands out to your sides.**

**Is your partner shooting? If yes, put your hands up in the air.**

Do this until you have the hang of it. Then switch!

# VICTORY DANCE

**Pretend you're a star football player. When you score a touchdown, how would you celebrate? Come up with a fun victory dance! Now think about dropping an easy pass. How would you react to making this mistake?**

Get a partner. On a sheet of paper, write "drop the ball." On another, write "score." Hold up your signs one at a time. Your partner will follow the conditionals on the next page.

**Does the sign say "drop the ball"? If yes, look disappointed.**

**Does the sign say "score"? If yes, do a victory dance!**

Play for a couple of minutes, and then switch with your partner.

# GOOD CATCH!

**Baseball players make some incredible catches! Players in the field must decide what to do while the ball is in the air.**

Crumple a sheet of paper into a ball. Then find a partner to play catch. You can throw the ball high, low, or pass it on the floor. While you're playing, discuss the different moves you might make under certain conditions.

**A. Is the ball in the air? If yes, I should . . .**

**B. Is the ball on the ground? If yes, I should . . .**

**C. Is the ball high above my head? If yes, I should . . .**

**Answer options:**

- put my glove down
- put my glove up
- jump for the ball

Check your answers on page 29. What other things might you do to catch a ball?

# UP AND OVER

**In volleyball, starting with a good serve is important. If the ball goes over the net, the teams can keep playing. If it doesn't, the other team gets a point. The team also gets to serve on the next turn.**

The flowchart on the next page shows a conditional. This conditional tells the players what to do after a serve. Choose the correct answer for the blank space.

A. You can serve again.

B. Your team gets a point.

C. The other team gets a point and gets to serve next.

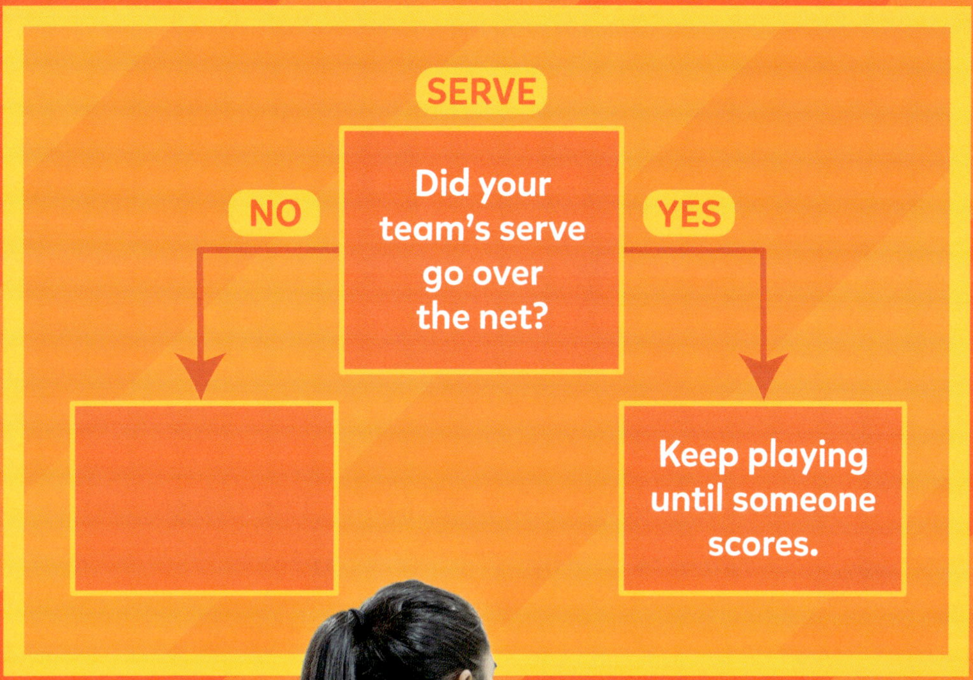
SERVE
Did your team's serve go over the net?
NO
YES
Keep playing until someone scores.

# BLOCK THAT SHOT!

**Imagine you're a soccer goalie. The other team is coming toward you fast! If they shoot, you'll block it. If they don't shoot, you'll stay ready.**

Copy the flowchart on page 15 onto a sheet of paper. Then fill in the blank boxes to help the goalie.

START

**Did the other team shoot?**

NO

YES

A. Move to block the shot

B. Stay still and watch the ball

# INTO THE END ZONE

**He could go all the way! In football, a touchdown is worth six points. You get three points if you make a field goal, and zero points if you miss. Touchdowns, field goals, and missed field goals are three of the conditions that decide a team's score.**

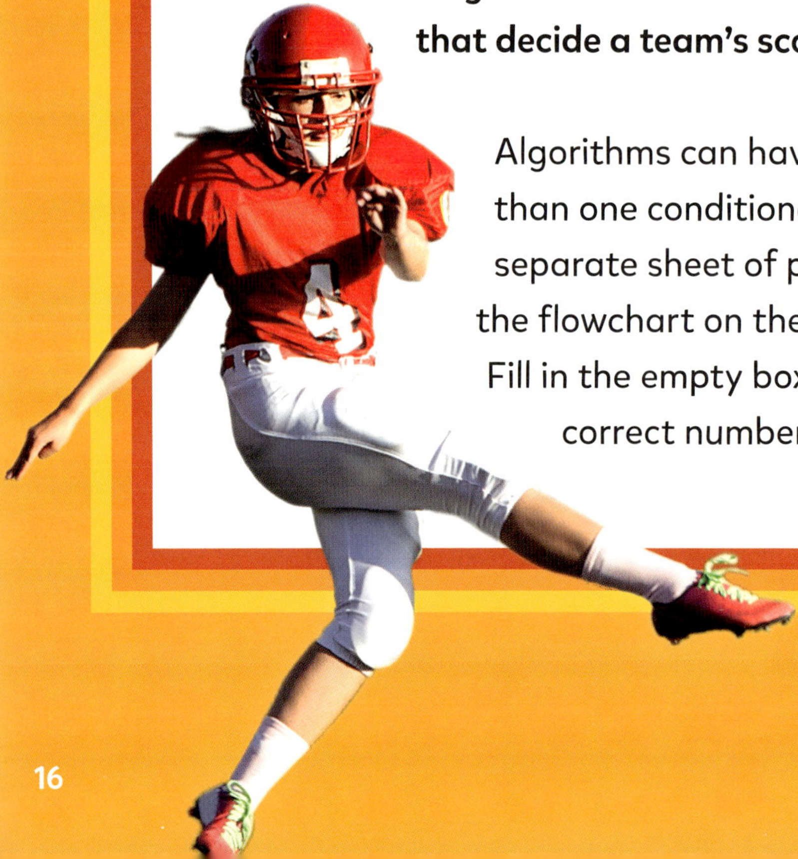

Algorithms can have more than one conditional too. On a separate sheet of paper, draw the flowchart on the next page. Fill in the empty boxes with the correct number of points.

PLAY
Did the team score a touchdown?
YES
__ Points
NO
Did the team make a field goal?
YES
__ Points
NO
__ Points

# LOOPED LEAPS

**Runners, get ready! There are five hurdles in this race. That means runners have to jump five times. Loops are lines of code that tell computers how many times to repeat an action. Conditionals can be loops too.**

Look at the looped conditional in the flowchart on the next page. Lay six sheets of paper in a row on the ground. Make sure they are at least a few feet apart. On a sixth sheet of paper, write "Finish Line." Pretend these sheets are your hurdles. Find a partner to read the conditional on the next page aloud to you. Then finish your race!

START
Run and jump
Are there more hurdles?
YES
NO
Cross the finish line.
Looped conditional

# THE WHITE FLAG IS UP!

**Race car drivers can use looped conditionals to finish races. When a race official waves a white flag, the driver in first place has one lap left!**

Turn a sheet of paper into your own white flag. On a different sheet, copy the flowchart on page 21 and fill in the correct answers. Have a partner run in a circle until you hold up the white flag. Then switch! Check your answer on page 29.

A. Finish the race!

B. Drive, drive, drive!

C. Is the white flag up?

# ON THE SLOPES

**Skiers zigzag down mountains—fast! But many things can get in their way.**

Imagine you're a ski instructor. Write an algorithm to teach your students how to get down the mountain safely. The flowchart on the next page includes possible dangers. First, decide how your skiers should react to each danger. Second, copy the flowchart onto a sheet of paper. Finally, fill in the blank spaces with your instructions.

SKI
Is there a person in your way?
YES
NO
Is there a hanging branch in your way?
YES
NO
Are you still on the mountain?
YES
NO
Relax, you're done!

# HIT OR MISS

**Step up to home plate! It's time to play a game of conditional baseball.**

The baseball field on page 27 is your game board. Grab a partner and a die and cut out eight small paper squares. These will be your players. You and your partner each get four players for your teams. Look at the conditional chart on page 26 to learn the rules of the game.

Play three innings with your partner. When the first game is over, make up your own rules. Draw a new flowchart and play again!

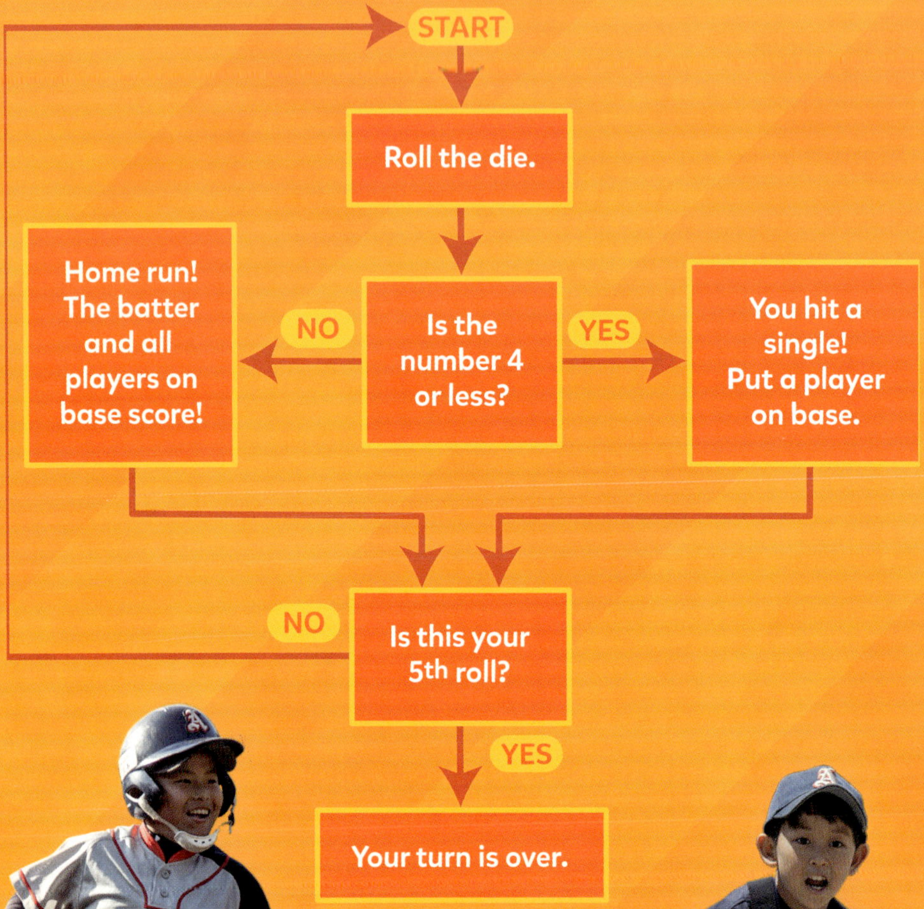
START
Roll the die.
Is the number 4 or less?
YES
You hit a single! Put a player on base.
NO
Home run! The batter and all players on base score!
Is this your 5th roll?
NO
YES
Your turn is over.

## Keep Coding

Sports are full of conditionals. Did a player pass, kick, or score? Each action a player takes decides what happens next. The way we act when we watch sports also depends on conditions. The next time you watch a game, observe how the people with you react to different conditions. Do they groan when the other team scores? Do they cheer when your team wins? What game conditions make them react the way they do?

You can notice conditionals in your daily life too. Did you do your homework? If you did, you can relax. If you did not, you need to get busy. Are you hungry? If you are, make a snack. If not, then wait for dinner. You can look for conditionals wherever you go!

# Answer Key

Page 10–11: A. Put my glove up. B. Put my glove down. C. Jump for the ball.

Pages 12–13: C. The other team gets a point and gets to serve next.

Pages 14–15: If the other team did not shoot, B. Stay still and watch the ball. If the team did shoot, then A. Move to block the shot.

Pages 16–17: If the team scored a touchdown, they get six points. If the team made the field goal, they get three points. If they did not make the field goal, they get zero points.

Pages 20–21: Start → B. Drive, drive, drive! → C. Is the white flag up? → If it is, A. Finish the race!

# Glossary

**algorithm:** a group of instructions made up of lines of code that tells a computer what to do

**code:** instructions written for computers to follow

**condition:** an occurrence that determines what happens next

**conditional:** a line of code that tells a computer what to do based on a certain condition

**dribble:** bouncing a basketball on the floor as you move

**field goal**: scoring three points by kicking the football through the goalpost

**loop:** a line of code that tells a computer to repeat an instruction a certain number of times

**pass:** to move the ball or puck from one teammate to another

**serve:** in volleyball, to hit the ball and begin play

**touchdown:** scoring six points for successfully crossing the opponent's end zone with the ball

# Further Information

Code.org: Conditionals
https://studio.code.org/s/course2/stage/12/puzzle/1

Coding: Conditionals
https://www.flocabulary.com/unit/coding-conditionals/

Funk, Josh. *How to Code a Sandcastle.* New York: Viking, 2018.

Loya, Allyssa. *Sporty Algorithms*. Minneapolis: Lerner Publications, 2020.

Lyons, Heather, and Elizabeth Tweedale. *Learn to Program*. Minneapolis: Lerner Publications, 2017.

Scratch Jr.
https://www.scratchjr.org/

# Index

algorithm, 4, 16, 22

code, 4, 18

conditionals, 4, 7–8, 12, 16, 18–19, 20, 24

conditions, 4, 10, 16

looped conditional, 18–19, 20

# Photo Acknowledgments

Image credits: Meg Oliphant/Getty Images, p. 4; Shoji Fujita/Getty Images, pp. 5 (pitcher), 25, 26 (both); J and J Productions/Getty Images, p. 5 (soccer); Francesco Carta fotografo/Getty Images, p. 5 (football); PBNJ Productions/Getty Images, p. 5 (basketball); FogStock/Vico Images?Alin Dragulin/Getty Images, p. 5 (vollyball); Icon Sportswire/Getty Images, pp. 6, 20; avid_creative/Getty Images, p. 6 (athlete); Carolyn Plummer/EyeEm/Getty Images, p. 7 (hoop); AR0795-001/Getty Images, p. 7 (athletes); TerryJ/Getty Images, pp. 8, 27; undefined undefined/Getty Images, p. 9 (football); aabejon/Getty Images, p. 10 (athlete); Rinek/Getty Images, p. 10 (glove); ; Megan Maloy/Getty Images, p. 11 (left); Yamada Taro/Getty Images, p. 11 (right); creativepictures/Getty Images, p. 12; FatCamera/Getty Images, p. 13; Laura Westlund/Independent Picture Service, pp. 13 (graphic), 15, 17, 19, 21, 23, 26, 27; David Blunsden/Getty Images, p. 14 (athlete); Glowimages/Getty Images, p. 14 (ball); Symphonie/Getty Images, p. 15; 3bugsmom/Getty Images, p. 16; Lawrence Manning/Getty Images, p. 17; Robin Skjoldborg/Getty Images, p. 18; FangXiaNuo/Getty Images, p. 19; mrPliskin/Getty Images, p. 21; yanik88/Getty Images, p. 22; TIZIANA FABI/Getty Images, p. 23; Jules Frazier/Getty Images, p. 24 (bat) David Lee/Shutterstock.com, p. 24 (glove); ronniechua/Getty Images, p. 24 (right).

Cover: Artur Didyk/Getty Images (hockey player), Yasser Chalid/Getty Images (basketball), Alexapicso/Shutterstock.com (football), Dan Thornberg/Shutterstock.com (baseball), kdshutterman/Shutterstock.com (soccer player), gremlin/Getty Images (background).

# About the Author

Allyssa Loya is an elementary school librarian in North Texas. She is the author of the Disney Coding Adventures series. Loya has two young boys. She is married to an IT manager, who is a perfect support system for her technological endeavors.